STUDY SKILLS FOR LIFE

A **CORRESPONDENCE COURSE** is
available for this book.
Call 1-877-75LEARN ext 2720 to order!

BUY & STUDY
How to Use a Dictionary
in order to increase comprehension
and gain the RIGHT tools to learn!

STUDY SKILLS FOR LIFE

Based on the Works of
L. RON HUBBARD

EFFECTIVE
EDUCATION
PUBLISHING

To the Student, Parent or Teacher

Important information about the usage of this book is written on pages 129–131. Your familiarity with and application of the data in that section can help you, your child or your students get more out of the book.

Published by
Effective Education Publishing
11755 Riverview Dr.
St. Louis, MO 63138

www.AppliedScholastics.org

ISBN 1-58460-055-1
© 1992, 1999, 2004
L. Ron Hubbard Library
All Rights Reserved

Printed in the United States of America

Contents

Introduction

1   Improving Your Ability to Learn   1

2   The Barriers to Study   11

     The First Barrier: Absence of Mass   13

     The Second Barrier: Too Steep a Gradient   27

     The Third—and Most Important—Barrier: The Misunderstood Word   42

3   Handling Misunderstood Words   63

4   The Use of Demonstration   79

     Demonstration and Learning   81

     Clay Demonstrations   84

     Sketching   94

5   Checkouts   97

Congratulations!   127

Important Information for Parents and Teachers   129

About the Author   133

For More Information   135

Introduction

Welcome to *Study Skills for Life*.

In this book you will learn HOW to learn anything you want. Whatever it is you want to learn, in school or out of school, you can learn IF you know how.

No one has ever taught you this before. You may remember your parents or teachers telling you to learn this, that or the other thing, but probably no one ever told you HOW to go about learning. And the truth is, no one knew it before.

Here's your chance.

Good luck!

Chapter One:

Improving Your Ability to Learn

Improving Your Ability to Learn

It is a big world, but you can learn anything you want to about it. By "learning" we do not mean just getting facts crammed into your head. A fact is something that is known to be true. Getting more and more facts is not learning.

Learning is understanding new things and getting better ways to do things in life. Those who get along well in life never really stop studying and learning.

The good engineer keeps up with new ways. The skilled athlete continually reviews the progress of his sport. Any professional person keeps a stack of books near at hand and refers to them often.

But before you can learn about something you have to want to learn about that thing.

If you think you already know all there is to know about something, you will not be able to learn about it.

The first thing you have to decide is that you want to learn something.

Is there something you want to learn?

Once you have decided on something, the next step is to study it. What is study? Study is the act or process of learning something. It is a careful examination of something. The word originally meant "eagerness."

The only reason for studying something is to be able to apply what you have studied. There really isn't any other good reason for being educated. Many people think they study only so they can pass a test. That is not a very good reason for studying. If you studied something so you could **do** something in life, that would be a worthwhile reason for studying. If you wanted to learn how to repair tractors you would study this subject with the goal of being able to repair a tractor.

It has been discovered that there is a way to study anything so that when you have studied it, you can apply what you have learned. Like being able to dance or play basketball or sing or fix a car, being able to study is an ability.

In this book you are going to learn the keys to study. These are skills you will be able to use your whole life in anything you do. A person never really stops learning and once you know the information contained in this book you will have skills that will help you in anything you want to do.

So, do you want to learn how to learn?

Drill

Use a sheet of paper to write down your answers.

a. What is something you would really like to learn about?

b. How would it help you to learn about that?

c. What would you have to do to learn about that?

Chapter Two:

The Barriers to Study

The Barriers to Study

You may have had the experience of studying something and running into trouble. Maybe you even gave up trying to make sense of what you were studying.

If this has ever happened to you it means you ran into one of the barriers to study. Barriers are things that get in your way or stop your progress. There are three main barriers to being able to study any subject.

If you know and understand what these barriers are and what to do about them, your ability to study and learn can be greatly increased.

The First Barrier: Absence of Mass

The *mass* of a subject refers to the parts of that subject which are composed of matter and energy which exist in the real world. For example, if you were studying how to operate tractors, the *mass* would be an actual tractor. This is different than *words* about tractors or *ideas* about tractors or the *history* of tractors. The mass would be the tractor itself—the wheels, the motor, the seat, the steering wheel and all the other things that make up tractors.

If you are trying to learn a subject and you don't have the actual thing that you are studying about, it can be very difficult for you. Imagine trying to learn how to run a tractor without having a tractor there!

14

If the mass of a subject is absent, you can actually feel squashed.

It can make you feel bent,

sort of spinny,

sort of dead,

or bored

or even angry.

If you are studying how to do something and you don't have the mass of it, this will be the result.

If you are studying about tractors, words on a page or someone telling you about tractors is no substitute for having an actual tractor there.

Photographs or motion pictures are helpful because they at least give the hope of the mass of a tractor.

It is important to understand that trying to learn about something when you don't have the mass of it available can produce the reactions shown earlier.

If you were trying to learn all about tractors but no one would show you any tractors or let you experience the mass of a tractor, you could wind up with a face that felt squashed, with headaches and with your stomach feeling funny. You might feel dizzy from time to time and often your eyes would hurt.

This knowledge is very useful. For example, if you were studying something and felt sick and it was traced back to a lack of mass, the way to fix this would be to supply the mass—the object itself or a reasonable substitute—and your sickness could rapidly clear up.

This barrier to study—the studying of something without its mass being around—produces some very definite reactions as we have seen. Now that you know this, do the following drills.

Drill

Write down how you would handle these situations:

a. You just got a new stereo for your birthday. You are reading the manual that came with it but you start to feel sort of spinny and bent. The stereo is still in the box. What do you do?

b. Your friend is reading about motorcycles but has no idea what they look like. There are no motorcycles nearby to show him. What could you use instead?

Drill

Write down how you could get mass if you were studying about the ocean.

The Second Barrier: Too Steep a Gradient

A *gradient* is a slope upwards or downwards. A flight of stairs is an easy gradient up to the higher floors of a building. Trying to reach the upper floors by climbing up the outside wall of the building would be a steep gradient and impossible to do.

Learning something is best done with a gradual approach, step by step, level by level. When you learn on a gradient, you learn a little bit more and a little bit more. Finally, you can easily do things which would have been too complex or difficult in the beginning of your studies in an area.

The best approach to learning something is a gradient approach where you learn things step by step.

When a person hits too steep a gradient in studying a subject there is a confusion which results. The person can feel like he is reeling or swaying. This is the second barrier to study.

Gradients are most applicable in the field of doingness or actions.

Say you were to find a person who was learning to fix engines and he was confused and sort of reeling.

You would know that there had been too much of a jump from one step of learning to fix engines to the next step. For example, learning to fix a simple engine and then learning to fix a more complicated type of engine. The person did not really understand something about the first type of engine but jumped to the next type of engine and this was too steep a gradient for him.

The person assigns all of his difficulties to the
new type of engine.

But the difficulty really lies at the tail end of learning to fix the first engine, the engine he felt he understood.

The remedy for too steep a gradient is to cut back the gradient. Find out when the person was not confused on the gradient and then find out what new action he undertook to do. Find out what he felt he understood well just *before* he got all confused.

You will find that there is something in this area—the area where he felt he understood it—which he did not really understand.

When this is cleared up, the person will be able to progress again.

SIMPLE ENGINE

MORE COMPLICATED ENGINE

This barrier of too steep a gradient is most easily seen when you are learning to *do* something. If you were just learning how to ride a motorcycle and someone demanded that you ride down a ramp and jump over a line of cars it would be very obvious that you had hit too steep a gradient.

When a person is found to be terribly confused on the second action he was supposed to do, it is a sure bet that he never really understood the *first* action.

Drill

Write down how you would handle this situation:

You are learning to dive. You have just learned to dive in the water from the side of the pool but you want to dive from the highest diving board ten feet off the water. What could you do to learn this at a proper gradient?

Drill

Write down a time you saw someone hit too steep a gradient. Describe what occurred. How could you have handled this using the data in this section of the book?

The Third — and Most Important — Barrier: The Misunderstood Word

The third and most important barrier to study is the *misunderstood word*.

"Mis" means *not* or *wrongly*.

"Misunderstood" means *not understood* or *wrongly understood*.

A misunderstood word is a word which is *not understood* or a word which is *wrongly understood*.

It does not matter if the word is a big word:

alphabetical

or a little word:

him.

If you read past a word which you do not understand you can get some bad reactions. These are different from the reactions that can occur with the first two barriers to study.

Reading on past a word that was not understood . . .

can make you feel blank or washed out.

It can make you feel "not there"

and a sort of nervous upset feeling can follow after that.

The confusion or inability to understand or learn comes AFTER a word that you did not have defined and understood.

Later . . .

A misunderstood definition or an undefined word can cause a person to give up studying a subject entirely and leave a course or class. Leaving in this way is called a "blow."

A person does not necessarily "blow" because of the other barriers to study—lack of mass or too steep a gradient. These barriers simply produce physical reactions. But the misunderstood word can cause a student to blow.

54

The misunderstood word is much more important than the other two barriers to study. The misunderstood word is what determines a person's ability to learn or understand quickly. People have been trying to test this for years but they did not know what it was.

It was simply the misunderstood word.

The misunderstood word is all that many study difficulties go back to. It is the misunderstood word that is the biggest factor involved with stupidity and many other things.

For example, if a person is not able to do things in the field of art, then there is some word that the person did not define or understand. This is followed by an inability to *do* things in the field of art.

This is very important because it tells you what can happen to a person's ability to do things in life. If he has misunderstood words, he may give up learning a subject or give up doing something. But it is more important to know that all you have to do to restore a person's ability to do something in life or to study something is to find the words he has misunderstood and get those words understood.

This is very simple technology.

The discovery of the misunderstood word actually opens the door to really becoming educated. And although this one has been given last, it is by far the most important of the barriers to study.

Drill

Write down how you would handle these situations:

a. You are reading a book. You get to the bottom of the page and realize that you don't remember any of what was written on the page. What should you do?

b. You do not feel like going back to class. Why might this be? How should you handle it?

Chapter Three:

Handling Misunderstood Words

Handling Misunderstood Words

When you come across a word you do not understand, it is important that you clear it up right away.

A misunderstood word will remain misunderstood until you "clear" the meaning of the word. "Clear" means to make understood. It means to learn the meaning of something. Once a word is fully understood, it is said to be "cleared."

Even a symbol can be misunderstood and must be cleared up. Imagine trying to work out the simple arithmetic problem 2 + 2 = ? if you did not know what 2, +, = and ? meant.

There are certain steps you take in order to clear up a misunderstood word. This is an important skill and once you have learned it, it is something that will stay with you always and is a skill you will rely on for the rest of your life.

How to Clear a Word

1. Have a dictionary nearby while reading so that you can clear any misunderstood word or symbol you come across. A simple but good dictionary can be found that does not use hard-to-understand words in the definitions.

2. When you come across a word or symbol that you do not understand, the first thing to do is get a dictionary and look up the word. Look rapidly over the definitions to find which one fits the way the word is being used in what you are reading. Read that definition.

LEG 1.

2. THE PART OF YOUR CLOTHES THAT COVERS A LEG. 3.

LEG

Now make up sentences using the word in that way until you have a clear idea of that meaning of the word. You may have to make up ten or more sentences until you get a really clear idea of that meaning of the word. That is okay. The important thing is for you to really understand the meaning of the word.

THE INK SPILLED ALL OVER THE LEG OF HER PANTS.

HE TORE THE LEG ON THE FENCE.

SHE USED SOME RED CLOTH TO PATCH UP THE LEG OF HER PANTS.

3. Now clear each of the other definitions of that word, using each one in sentences until you clearly understand each definition.

When a word has several different definitions, you cannot limit your understanding of the word to one definition only and call the word "understood." You must be able to understand the word later when you read it again and it is being used in a different way.

When you are clearing up a word you do not have to clear the technical or specialized definitions such as a specialized mathematics definition for the word or a technical definition from a branch of science, etc.

Sometimes a dictionary gives definitions of a word that are no longer used. These are called "obsolete" definitions and you do not have to clear those.

Also, some dictionaries give definitions of words that were used in ancient times and which are no longer used by people. These are called "archaic" definitions and you do not have to clear those.

The only time you would have to clear a specialized or technical or obsolete or archaic definition is when it is being used that way in what you were reading when you came across it.

4. The next thing to do is to clear the derivation of the word. The derivation is the explanation of where the word came from originally. This will help you to get a basic understanding of the word.

5. Sometimes words are used in ways that cannot be understood simply from the ordinary meanings of the words. For example, you might read the phrase "all in" in the sentence "Joe did not want to go to the party because he was feeling all in." You cannot figure out what is meant by the phrase "all in" simply by looking up "all" and "in." You have to look up the phrase itself and in this case it would be found under the word "all" in the dictionary and it means "very tired." When words are used this way, it is called an "idiom." There are many idioms in the language. When you say to a friend, "Joe is up to his neck in trouble" you mean that Joe is in a lot of trouble. It does not actually have anything to do with his neck.

If the word you are clearing has idioms, you do clear these as well.

6. If there is any other information given about the word such as a note on the usage of the word, be sure to read and understand this.

If words are listed which mean nearly the same thing as the word you are clearing be sure to read and understand these as well. These are called "synonyms." For instance, after the definition of the word "large" the dictionary might list "big," "huge," "great" and "tremendous" as synonyms.

All this other information will help to give you a full understanding of the word.

7. While clearing a word, if you find a misunderstood word or symbol in the definition, you should clear it right away using the procedure in steps 1–6 above. When this is done, return to the definition you were clearing. (The symbols and abbreviations used in the dictionary are usually given in the front of the dictionary.)

If you find yourself spending a lot of time clearing words within definitions of words, you should get a simpler dictionary. A good dictionary will enable you to clear a word without having to look up a lot of other words while doing that.

Anytime you are reading or studying and the material becomes hard to grasp, or you can't seem to understand what you are reading or you feel blank, washed out or feel like throwing the book down, *realize that you have gone past a misunderstood word*. Don't go any further, but go back to just *before* you got into difficulty, find the misunderstood word and clear it.

Once you have looked up the word and fully understood it, then restudy the book from that point. It should now be easy to understand. If it isn't, there is another word that you don't understand. You must find it and get it looked up and fully understood.

Knowing the steps of how to clear a word is one of the most important parts of learning. Once you know how to clear a word there is no word you cannot understand.

Drill

Practice the steps of clearing up a word until you know the steps of doing this and can do them easily. Do this with the words "home," "shoe" and "chimney."

Drill

Remember a word or find a word you know you do not understand or are unsure of and clear it using a dictionary.

Drill

Go back through the section "Handling Misunderstood Words" and look for any words you do not fully understand. Clear these in the dictionary and restudy the section as you go. Write down what words you found and cleared.

Chapter Four:

The Use of Demonstration

Demonstration and Learning

The word *demonstration* means "the act or process of showing something or of showing how something operates or works." It comes from the Latin word *demonstrare*, which means "to point out, show, prove."

Demonstrating things has a lot of use in learning. It shows whether or not someone really understands what he is studying or if he can apply what he has learned.

In studying, a student can do a "demonstration" or "demo" with something called a "demo kit." A demo kit consists of various small objects such as corks, caps, paper clips, pen tops, rubber bands, etc. The student uses his hands and the pieces of his demo kit to demonstrate an idea or principle.

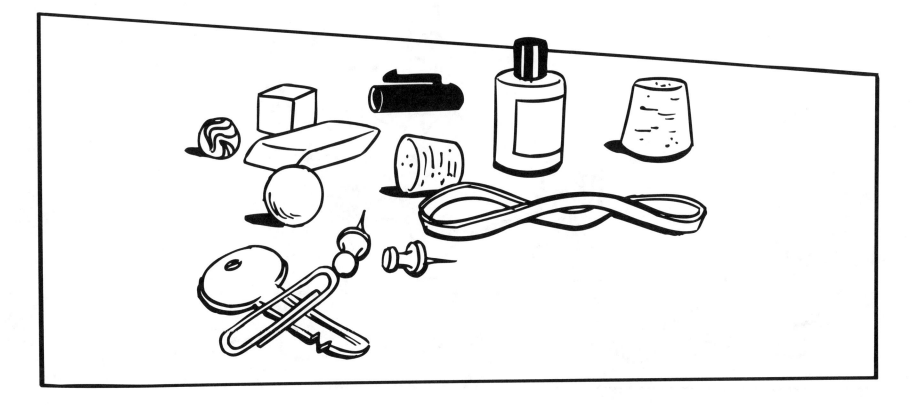

If a student ran into something he couldn't quite figure out, a demo kit would assist him to understand it. By making the different pieces of the demo kit represent the objects he is studying about, the student can move them around and see more clearly how they relate to each other, etc.

By doing demonstrations of what he is studying, the student is getting mass to go along with the ideas studied.

OKAY, THIS IS SUE, AND SHE GOES OVER TO THE CORNER AND . .

Drill

Using your demo kit, demonstrate the following things about the barriers to study which you have learned about earlier in this book:

a. How you would recognize that you had lack of mass and how you would handle this.

b. How you would recognize that you were at too steep a gradient and how you would handle this.

c. How you would know you have misunderstood word and how you would handle this.

Clay Demonstrations

Another form of demonstration is using clay figures to demonstrate a concept or principle. These are called clay demonstrations or clay demos. Clay demos can help you understand better what you are studying. Doing clay demos accomplishes several things:

1. They make the materials being studied real to the student by making him DEMONSTRATE them in clay.

2. They give a proper balance of mass and significance.

3. Clay demos teach the student to apply.

If you come across something you cannot figure out, you can work it out in clay.

How to Do a Clay Demo

In doing a clay demo, the clay gives mass. Then a label is added to each piece of clay in the demonstration that says what the thing is.

Say you wanted to do a clay demo of a pencil. First, make a thin roll of clay. This is the pencil lead.

You would make a label using a strip of paper and write on it with a pen "LEAD" and stick it on the thin roll of clay.

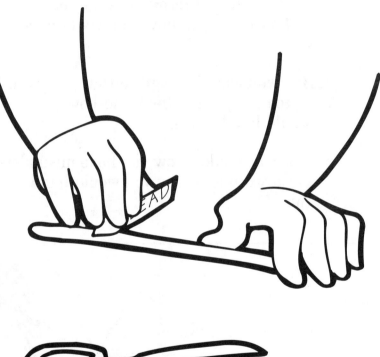

Next, put on another layer of clay with the thin roll sticking out a little bit at one end. This is the wood part of the pencil, so you would make a label that said "WOOD" and stick it on.

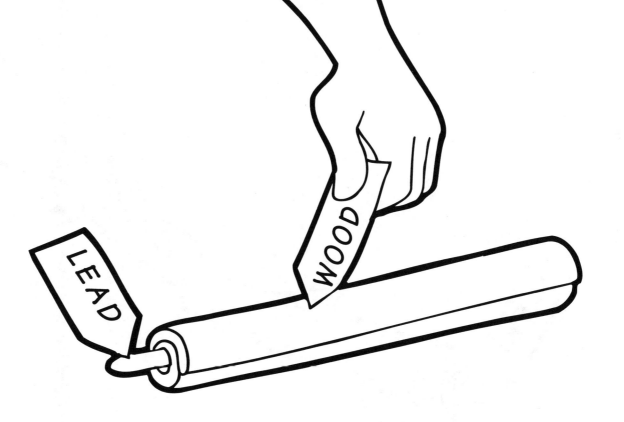

Then you put another little piece of clay on the end. This is the rubber eraser so you would write "RUBBER" on a label and stick it on that piece of clay.

Finally, you make a label for the whole thing,
"PENCIL."

88

You could show someone you understand something by removing the overall label and then getting another person to examine your clay demo. He would just look and figure out what you had demonstrated. If he could tell what you were demonstrating just from the clay and without asking you any questions and with you not saying anything, that would show that you understood what you had studied well enough to demonstrate it in clay to another person.

90

Clay Demo Size

Clay demos must be large.

One of the purposes of clay demonstrations is to make the materials being studied real to a person. If your clay demo is small (less mass), it may not provide enough mass for you. And long experience has shown that BIG clay demos are more successful in helping to increase understanding.

Making the parts of a clay demo artistic is not important. The forms can be crude.

Labeling Clay Demonstrations

Each separate thing is labeled that is part of a clay demonstration, no matter how crude the label is. Students usually do labels with scraps of paper written on with a ballpoint. When cutting out a label, a point is put on one end, making it easy to stick the label into the clay.

Each time you make an object you label it. You make the first object of your clay demo, label it, make the second object, label it, make the third object, label it and so on.

Anything can be demonstrated in clay. You can even show a thought. Use a thin ring of clay to show a thought or idea. Here is a clay demo of a person thinking about a ball.

If you don't understand something in life or in what you are studying, you can work it out in clay and understand it better. Clay demos are an important part of good study skills.

Drill

Use a sheet of paper to write down your answer.

How could you use clay demos to help you understand something better? Give an example of something specific.

Sketching

Sketching is also part of demonstration and part of working things out.

Someone sitting at his desk trying to work something out may not have any clay to hand to work it out with, but he could work it out with a paper and pencil, and draw a picture of it or a graph of it. This would help him understand it better.

An obvious example is a ship's navigator who, instead of trying to work it all out in her head with some foggy concept of where she is simply graphs the sailing plan and progress on a chart.

Drill

Use sketching to do a demonstration of a student clearing a misunderstood word.

Chapter Five:

Checkouts

Checkouts

A checkout is the action of examining a student's knowledge of the material he is studying. This is an excellent way of seeing whether someone understands what he has studied.

If you give someone a checkout on something he has studied you will be able to see if he really understands what he's studied

It will never do a student any good in life to *know* some facts. The student is expected to *use* facts.

Therefore, it is important to remember that all checkouts must test the student's understanding of what he has studied.

A proper checkout is not a test of whether someone can memorize what he has read and repeat it back. That is no proof that he understands and can apply what he has studied.

Example of a Checkout

Say you want to check out a friend on the manual which tells him how to operate his new motorcycle.

Go over the first part of the material you are checking him out on and pick out a few uncommon words. Ask him to define each and demonstrate its use in a made-up sentence. If he couldn't define the words or use them in sentences you would know he does not understand his materials well. He would "flunk" the checkout and would have to look up the words he did not understand and restudy his materials.

You would have to make sure that you also know what the words mean before you start to check him out.

When your friends shows he understands the words, you ask him questions about the materials that get him to show he understands how the materials are applied. Questions like, "Now this rule here about always wearing a helmet while riding, how come there'd be such a rule?" If he couldn't imagine why, you would send him back to the words just before that rule to find the one he hadn't grasped.

In a checkout, the person must show that he understands the words and understands how the materials are applied.

Giving Checkouts

A correct checkout is done only by making the person being tested answer:

a. The meanings of the words (redefining the words used in his own words and demonstrating their use in his own made-up sentences), and

b. Demonstrating how the data is used.

Checkouts must include demonstrations of the materials using a demo kit. In a checkout, you should ask questions that require an ability to *apply* the material. Give the person you are checking out a situation and have him tell you how he would handle it.

Before any person may give another a checkout, he must himself have read the material. If he is checking out someone on a taped lecture, he must have listened to the lecture. This will make it possible to give a good checkout.

This is not a checkout!

This is an example of a correct checkout.

When the checkout of the words is completed, a checkout is done on the materials.

Here's what to do if you flunk a checkout:

Being able to do a good checkout is an important study skill. You can tell if a person really understands something by giving him a checkout on it.

Drill

a. Find another student or a friend to do this drill with. Get a copy of something that both of you have studied and are familiar with. (If there are no materials which you have both studied, then choose something for use in the drill and both of you study it.) Ask the person irrelevant questions about this material and demand that he quote certain sentences and phrases from it word for word. Write down what you did and what occurred.

b. Now give the other person a standard checkout on the above materials, using the data in this chapter. Write down what you did and what occurred.

CONGRATULATIONS!

You have completed *Study Skills for Life*.

The skills you have learned, if you use them, can help you greatly in anything you want to do in life. A person never really stops learning and knowing how to study is something you can use every day. It is very well done that you have accomplished this.

The real benefit of your new study skills comes when you apply them. Whatever you want to learn in life, you can learn it faster and better by using what you learned in this book.

Important Information for Students, Parents and Teachers

This book has been published to fill an important need.

We live now in an instruction-book world. Our civilization is highly technical.

Formal education today goes into one's twenties, nearly a third of a lifetime. But what happens when a person leaves school? Can he *do* what he studied? And factually, education begins *before* a person learns to speak and continues throughout his entire life. Can he *do* what he has studied outside of the classrooms of his school days?

Any young person's future success and happiness are dependent on his ability to learn. Innately, this ability is very strong. Young children, for instance, possess an almost boundless fascination about everything in life. A curiosity and eagerness to explore and learn is turned on "high" at a very young age.

Young people are confronted with so many things they don't yet understand. They have been told that learning is the key to their future. But it is a mean trick to tell someone that he must learn and then not teach him the skills he needs to enable him to learn.

Study Skills for Life contains fundamental principles of L. Ron Hubbard's researches into the field of education, where he isolated the basics which underlie all forms of learning. His breakthroughs resulted in Study Technology, the first subject which actually deals with HOW to learn. Study Technology is basic to any specific subject since it deals with learning itself, the barriers to learning and remedies for these barriers.

Study Skills for Life presents the fundamentals of Study Technology at a level that a young person can assimilate, understand and *use*. It is a breakthrough in the field of learning and education for preteenagers and teenagers.

Using the Book for Maximum Benefit

Reading Level

The book is written so that a person can study it by himself. It has been written for young adults and includes people younger than twelve who have successfully used the book.

Drills

There are drills throughout the book which get the reader to *apply* what he has read. These are key to gaining the most from the book and the student should be encouraged to do them thoroughly.

Familiarity

In working with a son or daughter on the book or in using it in a classroom, it will help if you have read the book first and are familiar with its contents. Though simply written, the data presented here are not to be found in any previously published book on education or learning. The concepts are totally original with the researches of L. Ron Hubbard into the field of education and his discoveries on the mental phenomena which block learning, the physiological manifestations which result from these blocks and the specific remedies for each one.

Ensuring Understanding

In giving this book to your son or daughter and in working with him or her on the book or in using it in a classroom situation, there is one very important datum about study of which you should be aware:

THE ONLY REASON A PERSON GIVES UP A STUDY OR BECOMES CONFUSED OR UNABLE TO LEARN IS BECAUSE HE HAS GONE PAST A WORD THAT WAS NOT UNDERSTOOD.

The confusion or inability to grasp or learn comes AFTER a word that the person did not have defined and understood.

Have you ever had the experience of coming to the end of a page and realizing you didn't know what you had read? Well, somewhere earlier on that page you went past a word that you had no definition for or an incorrect definition for.

Here's an example. "It was found that when the crepuscule arrived the children were quieter and when it was not present, they were livelier." You see what happens. You think you don't understand the whole idea, but the inability to understand came entirely from the one word you could not define, crepuscule, which means twilight or darkness.

The datum about not going past an undefined word is the most important datum in study and is thoroughly covered in the book on pages 42–60. Every subject a person has taken up and then abandoned or done poorly at had its words which the person failed to get defined. It is the most important barrier to study and a parent or teacher should be familiar with this datum. The phenomena which occur after a person has unknowingly encountered a word he or she did not understand are quite distinct and easily recognized once you know what you are looking at.

As simple as it seems, many of the tribulations in students' lives can be traced back to words they have not understood in their study materials or in life.

Use as a Reference Book

After someone has read the book and learned these study skills, he can and should be referred back to his materials whenever necessary during his future studies. As startling as it may seem, a workable technology of how to study something was foreign to the field of education before L. Ron Hubbard's researches in the area. *Study Skills for Life* can be used time and time again as a reminder of the basics of successful learning.

Further Information

Numerous schools across the United States and throughout the world now utilize Mr. Hubbard's Study Technology to promote faster learning with increased comprehension.

If you or your child or student encounter any difficulties in reading or applying the data in this book there are addresses of schools and institutions on our website "www.AppliedScholastics.org" you can contact. These organizations make exclusive use of Study Technology and will be happy to provide any assistance needed as well as provide further information about these new advances in education.

There is also a toll-free number you can call for assistance or for further information: (1-800-424-5397).

When a person knows how to gain more knowledge, his enthusiasm for learning will never become stale. Once a person grasps the tools contained here these will become a natural part of his approach to living and he will use them throughout all his activities in life.

The fundamentals contained in *Study Skills for Life* are sweeping discoveries in the field of education and they open the gates to learning and application.

When a person has learned how to learn, all knowledge becomes available to him, assuring that, whatever his fields of interest, he will have the greatest possible chance for fulfillment and success.

About the Author

L. Ron Hubbard was no stranger to education. Although his main profession was that of a professional writer, in a long, event-filled and productive life he spent thousands of hours researching in the education field, lecturing and teaching.

He was born in Tilden, Nebraska on March 13, 1911, and his early years were spent on his grandfather's ranch in the wilds of Montana. As the son of a us Navy commander, he was well on the way to becoming a seasoned traveler by the age of eight, and by the time he was nineteen he had logged over a quarter of a million miles.

He enrolled in George Washington University in 1930, taking classes in mathematics and engineering. But his was not a quiet academic life. He took up flying in the pioneer days of aviation, learning to pilot first glider planes and then powered aircraft. He worked as a freelance reporter and photographer. He directed expeditions to the Caribbean and Puerto Rico, and later, to Alaska. The world was his classroom and he studied voraciously, gathering experience which provided the background for his later writings, research and discoveries.

Some of his first published articles were nonfiction, based upon his aviation experience. Soon he began to draw from his travels to produce a wide variety of fiction stories and novels: adventure, mystery, westerns, fantasy and science fiction.

The proceeds from his fiction writing funded his main line of research and exploration—how to improve the human condition. His nonfiction works cover such diverse subjects as drug rehabilitation, marriage and family, success at work, statistical analysis, public relations, art, marketing and much, much more. But he did more than write books—he also delivered over 3,000 lectures and conducted courses to impart his own discoveries to others.

However, in order to learn, one must be able to read and understand. Therefore, L. Ron Hubbard tackled the problem of teaching others how to study. His research uncovered the basic reason for the failure of a student to grasp any subject. He discovered the barriers to full comprehension of what one is studying, and developed methods by which anyone can improve his ability to learn and to *apply* the data that he is being taught. He wrote a considerable body of work on this subject, which he termed *Study Technology*.

L. Ron Hubbard's advanced technology of study is now used by an estimated three million students and thousands of teachers in universities and school systems internationally. His educational materials have been translated into more than eighteen languages to meet this worldwide demand for the first truly *workable* technology of how to study. Organizations delivering L. Ron Hubbard's Study Technology have been established in over 60 countries around the world.

L. Ron Hubbard departed this life on January 24, 1986. His contributions to the world of education have meant new hope, better understanding and increased ability for millions of students and educators the world over.

For more information on educational books and materials by L. Ron Hubbard, go to www.AppliedScholastics.org or contact your nearest distributor:

Applied Scholastics International
11755 Riverview Dr.
St. Louis, MO 63138
877-75LEARN
www.AppliedScholastics.org

Eastern United States
(727) 432-3233
EMAIL:
EUSContRep@APPLIEDSCHOLASTICS.ORG

Western United States
(714) 348-9162
EMAIL:
WUSContRep@APPLIEDSCHOLASTICS.ORG

Canada
Applied Scholastics Canada
678 Pape Ave, Toronto
Ontario M4K 3S4 Canada
416-463-9950
EMAIL:
APSCANADA@APPLIEDSCHOLASTICS.ORG

Europe
Applied Scholastics Europe
Nørregade 26
Copenhagen K 1165 Denmark
45 33 32 3680
EMAIL:
APSEU@APPLIEDSCHOLASTICS.ORG

South Africa
Education Alive Africa
A4, Crowthorne Shopping Centre
Corner of Main & Arthur Roads
Crowthorne, Midrand 1684
South Africa
2711 702 2208
EMAIL:
APSAF@APPLIEDSCHOLASTICS.ORG

Australia
Applied Scholastics Australia,
   New Zealand, Oceania
89 Jones Street, Suite 64
Ultimo, NSW 2007 Australia
612 928 01023
EMAIL:
APSANZO@APPLIEDSCHOLASTICS.ORG

England
Applied Scholastics UK
27 Balls Green, Withyham,
E. Sussex TN7 4BU England
44 189 277 0949
EMAIL:
APSUK@APPLIEDSCHOLASTICS.ORG

Latin America
Applied Scholastics Latin America
Miguel Angel de Quevedo 871
Colonia Los Reyes Coyoacan
México D.F. 04330 México
52 55 5211 8452
EMAIL:
APSLATAM@APPLIEDSCHOLASTICS.ORG

You can also contact any of the international groups and organizations which use L. Ron Hubbard's Study Technology by going to: **www.AppliedScholastics. org/locator.php**

Additional Books by L. Ron Hubbard

Learning How to Learn · For children, knowing how to read and being able to understand and apply what they read is the real key to success in their lives. With the simple steps taught in this book, written for young students, learning can become an exciting and rewarding experience.

Grammar and Communication · The ability to communicate is vital to happiness and self-confidence. But getting one's communication across is dependent upon being able to speak and write correctly. The unique approach to grammar taught in this book can open the world of words to a child—granting him the strong sense of self-esteem which results from the ability to read well, write clearly and communicate effectively.

How to Use a Dictionary · This book provides students with the means to get the most out of their education through the use of the dictionary. Students learn everything from finding words quickly to understanding the symbols in dictionaries. It opens doors for those who would otherwise be unable to understand even the simplest of terms.

Basic Study Manual · Whether you're going to college or starting a career, you need the ability to apply anything that you study, so you can do what you want in life. Using these skills, you can improve your concentration, improve your ability to learn and enjoy what you are studying.

All of these books are available as correspondence courses.

When a person can learn and think for himself/herself the world is an open book.